CELEBRATE THE SEASONS!

by
PHYLLIS STANLEY
and
MILTINNIE YIH

NAVPRESS
A MINISTRY OF THE NAVIGATORS
P.O. Box 6000, Colorado Springs, Colorado 80934

The Navigators is an international Christian organization. Jesus Christ gave His followers the Great Commission to go and make disciples (Matthew 28:19). The aim of The Navigators is to help fulfill that commission by multiplying laborers for Christ in every nation.

NavPress is the publishing ministry of The Navigators. NavPress publications are tools to help Christians grow. Although publications alone cannot make disciples or change lives, they can help believers learn biblical discipleship, and apply what they learn to their lives and ministries.

© 1986 by Phyllis Stanley and Miltinnie Yih
All rights reserved, including translation
ISBN: 0-89109-116-5
11163

Second printing, 1987

Cover illustration by Ken Westphal

Printed in the United States of America

CONTENTS

AUTHORS

Phyllis Stanley is a wife and the mother of four children. She and her husband, Paul, were Navigator missionaries for eleven years in Europe. They now live in Colorado Springs, where Phyllis continues to lead women's Bible studies and Paul is the Eastern Divisional Director of United States Ministries for The Navigators.

Miltinnie Yih is a wife and the mother of three children. She and her husband, Lee, are associated with Personal Development Foundation and live in Hong Kong, where Miltinnie leads women's Bible studies.

PREFACE

The word holiday comes from the phrase "holy day," which means a special day set aside for spiritual or religious purposes. In our times, however, holidays often seem empty and commercialized. Retailers and greeting card companies schedule our lives around holidays in order to capitalize on them for financial gain.

How we long for *true* meaning instead of mere sentimentality! We are dissatisfied with the cheap substitutes offered to us, yet we are frustrated by not knowing how to introduce meaningful spiritual truths into our own lives and the lives of those around us.

We've written these studies to help provide a scriptural basis for turning holidays into special times of focusing on Him for whom the holy days were made. Many holidays give us the opportunity to study and celebrate some of the greatest doctrines and biblical emphases of our faith: the Incarnation, the Cross, the Resurrection, love, renewal, thankfulness, and fruitfulness.

Because we have become a transient society of people who move often and have family members scattered around the world, many of us do not have deep geographical roots. However, spiritual celebrations of holidays can root our faith in God, who never changes. Thus, we gather in a circle around His Word to celebrate the great things that God has done for us so that we can put our confidence in Him and remember

5

His works throughout the year (Psalm 78:7).

These studies can be used in Bible study groups, Sunday school classes, one-on-one studies, and family devotions. They can also be used in personal times alone with the Lord as you prepare your heart and mind for the coming of a special season. You are better prepared to share spiritual truths with those closest to you when you communicate what is stored in your heart.

The suggestions for group activities that we've included are designed to supplement the studies, but they can also be used in place of sections of the longer studies. Try them around your family table, with friends in your home, or as a Bible study wrap-up treat. Consider them opportunities for more focused fellowship—meaningful sharing and mutual caring.

As you, your family, and your friends weave the love of Jesus Christ and His Word into special holiday times, we pray that your lives will be enriched as your roots go deeper into the wonderful truths of what God has done for you. And as you study throughout the year, may the rhythm of the holidays become the rhythm of a heart that seeks God not only in holidays but in mundane days as well, until all days become holy days dedicated to Him.

PHYLLIS STANLEY
MILTINNIE YIH

SEASONAL
BIBLE
STUDIES

THANKSGIVING
Counting Our Blessings

Thanksgiving is a time for remembering and praising God. It has become a special day for counting our blessings.

Although people of many countries observe a Thanksgiving celebration with special emphasis on the autumn harvest, America's Thanksgiving is woven into our country's dramatic earliest history. Looking back to our historical roots focuses our attention on our rich inheritance as free citizens of this country. Looking back on our *spiritual* heritage reminds us of the riches of God's grace, freely given to us as citizens of His Kingdom.

THE NATURE OF THANKSGIVING

After 66 days of a stormy voyage across the Atlantic Ocean, the Mayflower reached Plymouth on December 2, 1620. Although the shores were icy and the terrain bleak, the Pilgrims were thankful to have found a land of freedom where they could openly worship God. They spent their last day on the Mayflower in worship and thanksgiving. After a long, bitter-cold winter, spring came at last. The Pilgrims continued to thank God, but through many tears, for half of their community had died from sickness.

These early settlers were thankful to God at the outset of their adventure into the new country, during their settling, and through their difficulties. When the fruit of their hard work

9

and planting was harvested, their thankfulness climaxed in a great feast. From the bounty of their harvest, they gave thanks to God and initiated our Thanksgiving Day.

---

1. How would you define thankfulness?

---

2. Take a few minutes to reflect on what you are most thankful for in your life right now. Write down the kinds of things that come to your mind—perhaps in the form of a prayer you can offer to God.

---

3. Think about whatever makes it difficult for you to express thanks or to cultivate an attitude of thankfulness. What seem to be the chief reasons for such difficulty?

4. Look up Ephesians 5:20 and 1 Thessalonians 5:18.

   a. What is similar about Paul's instructions in these two
   verses?

   b. Notice the larger context for each of these verses: a series of specific commands for holy living. Why do you
   think Paul included thanksgiving in this series? What
   does this suggest to you about the nature of thanksgiving?

THE FOCUS OF THANKSGIVING

Thanksgiving was commanded by God all through the Old
Testament. The Israelites were to build booths, erect altars,
and establish monuments so that they would not forget to be
thankful for all God had done for them. They were to
remember God's protection, His provision, His greatness, and
His love.

5. a. In 1 Samuel 12:24, what did Samuel tell Israel to
   remember or consider?

11

b. Look back at 1 Samuel 12:6-11. What were the "great things" God had done for Israel that Samuel wanted the people to remember?

c. Why do you think Samuel wanted the people to focus on God's acts in the past?

6. a. What are some great things that God has done for you?

b. What are some ways that you might "remember" them during this Thanksgiving season?

The Psalms are filled with thanksgiving to God. Using selections from the Psalms as our own prayers to God can help us integrate thankfulness into our prayer life.

7. Read Psalm 103 slowly and thoughtfully.

a. List at least four of God's blessings for which David was thankful.

b. Are there any parts of this Psalm in which you can share David's feelings of thankfulness? If so, write down what they are and why you feel thankful.

c. Using your reflections on Psalm 103, write out your own prayer of thanksgiving to God.

Because God chooses to use other people as channels of blessing in our lives, we need to develop a thankfulness for others in our focus on what God has done for us. We can either take others for granted or develop an "attitude of gratitude" for people in our lives. But where does such thankfulness for our families, friends, and acquaintances begin?

8. a. In the following passages, what does Paul remember about his friends?

Philippians 1:3-6

1 Thessalonians 1:2-3

b. What is the context of Paul's recollections about these people? (Philippians 1:3-4, 1 Thessalonians 1:2).

14

c. What does Paul's attitude suggest about our intercession for others?

9. a. Have you ever experienced growth in thankfulness by praying for people in your life? If so, describe briefly one example.

b. List some personal thanks for friends, and then pray about them.

10. a. Think about those people who have played a significant role in your coming to Christ. Think also about those who have helped you grow deeper in God's Word. Who are those people who have given you time, friendship, or love? How can remembering their contribution to your life cause you to be thankful?

b. Is there anything that you feel you should do this week as a way of expressing your gratitude for them?

THE LASTING HARVEST OF THANKSGIVING

God is at home with the praise of His people (Psalm 22:3). When we praise and thank Him, He draws especially close to us with His presence, giving us confidence in trials and a sense of joy in our hearts.

11. a. Read Luke 17:11-19. Describe the setting and the miracle that Jesus performed.

b. For what did Jesus commend the leper who returned?

c. Why do you think the other lepers did not return?

d. What do you think the one leper who came back gained by returning?

CHOOSING TO GIVE THANKS

It is natural to grumble when situations are difficult; it is supernatural to thank God for what He is doing or what He is going to do.

12. The Pilgrims could have chosen a day of mourning instead of a day of thanksgiving. What do you think caused them to choose to be thankful?

When Corrie Ten Boom and her sister, Betsy, were transferred to the Ravensbruck concentration camp in Germany, they were horrified at the filthy conditions, soiled bedding, and ineffective plumbing. They had only straw beds to sleep on. They could not imagine at first how they would be able to endure sleeping and living in those conditions. Then they remembered the Bible verse, "Give thanks in all circumstances," and in faith they began to thank God that they were together, that they had a Bible, that because they were packed so closely together they could share God's Word. They even thanked God for the fleas. After praying in this way, they realized that the fleas were the very thing that kept the squeamish guards out of their room!

---

13. a. A spirit of thanksgiving can sometimes seem like a thin disguise for what is actually a naive approach to life, which glosses over difficulties and refuses to face reality. What do you think is the difference between a false spirit of thanks and a truly realistic one?

b. Do you think Corrie and Betsy were naive? Why or why not?

c. How did their choice affect them?

18

14. Read in 2 Chronicles 20:1-21 about the military challenge that was facing Jehoshaphat, king of Judah.

    a. What was the disturbing news that Jehoshaphat received? (verse 2).

    b. How did Jehoshaphat feel and what was his response? (verse 3).

    c. Look carefully at Jehoshaphat's prayer in 2 Chronicles 20:6-12. Sum up the major points in his prayer.

    d. What did Jehoshaphat do even before there was any answer to his prayer? (verses 20-21).

15. Are you in a situation now where you find it difficult to offer thanksgiving to God? If so, review your study in this lesson to reflect on verses or concepts that encourage you to *choose* to offer God a sacrifice of thanksgiving. Write down the passages or principles you've selected.

As we express thankfulness to God and to special people in our lives, we'll find the holiday season becoming more meaningful. It will become truly one of *thanksgiving* instead of *thankskeeping*.

"O LORD my God, I will give you thanks forever" (Psalm 30:12).

CHRISTMAS
God with Us

Advent is a time of preparation. The Old Testament prophets prepared. In the New Testament times their prophecies were carried to fulfillment in the birth of the Savior: "Prepare the way for the Lord" (Matthew 3:3).

And we are preparing for Christ's coming as well. We prepare our hearts as we seek to focus on the real meaning of Christmas: Jesus' life with us and in us.

We are preparing our homes to reflect our joy in this season—festive, warm, inviting.

And we are preparing gifts for loved ones in other places, and for a reunion with family members from whom we've been separated.

But we are not the only ones preparing. God has been preparing Christmas for us. He has gone to great lengths to establish a setting, a name, a prophet, and a woman—each incident a part of His unfolding plan to bring to us Someone to save us from our sins.

GOD PREPARED A SETTING

There are some 333 prophecies in the Old Testament concerning the birth, life, and death of the Messiah. The probability of that number of predictions finding their fulfillment in one person is astronomical—yet that is precisely what happened in the person of Jesus Christ. Read the following passages to uncover just two of those prophecies in the beginning of the Christmas story.

---

1. What did God do to prepare the place of the Messiah's birth? (Micah 5:2, Luke 2:1-5).

---

2. What was extremely unusual about the birth? (Isaiah 7:14, Luke 1:26-27,34).

---

3. What do Galatians 4:4 and Hebrews 1:1-2 indicate about the timing of Christ's coming?

---

4. What does David's statement in Psalm 31:15 indicate about the timing of events in our lives?

GOD PREPARED A NAME

Seven hundred years before the birth of Christ, Isaiah prophetically prepared Israel for the birth of the Messiah. Christ was born into a human nature so that He could understand and represent us. As the Son of God, He was the Father's greatest gift to the world. He came to save us.

5. What are some of the names that were prepared in advance for Jesus? (Isaiah 9:6-9).

6. Take a few minutes to reflect on the names you listed in the previous question. Select one name that seems particularly significant to you right now. Write down the characteristics of Jesus suggested by that title, and describe how those characteristics can meet a particular need in your life.

His name is *Wonderful*: this takes care of the *dullness* of life. We no longer need to live on the cheap substitutes of the world in order to have excitement and enjoyment. Jesus Christ makes everything wonderful.

His name is *Counselor*: this takes care of the *decisions* of life. We no longer will be baffled by the problems of life, wondering what step to take next. With Jesus Christ as our Counselor, we will have the wisdom that we need to make the right decision.

His name is *The Mighty God*: this takes care of the *demands* of life. And life is demanding! Sometimes we feel like giving up; but through Jesus Christ we can have the strength that we need to continue—and to conquer.

His name is *The Everlasting Father*: this takes care of the *dimensions* of life. We can become a part of eternity! A whole new dimension of living can be ours through Jesus Christ, when the government of our life is on His shoulders.

His name is *The Prince of Peace*: this takes care of the *disturbances* of life. How we long for lasting peace within! What we would not give for the secret of poise and confidence in a threatening world! The answer is— Jesus Christ. He is the Prince of Peace, and when He controls the government of your life, He gives you peace.

Warren Wiersbe
(*His Name Is Wonderful*, Tyndale House, 1976, page 17)

GOD PREPARED A PROPHET

7. In Mark 1:2-3, an Old Testament prophecy is quoted. What did it predict?

8. How did John the Baptist fulfill this prophecy quoted in Mark 1:2-3? (Matthew 11:10-14, Mark 1:4-8, John 1:19-36).

9. How did John's attitude and message prepare the way for Jesus?

10. Read John 3:28-30 and Acts 20:35. As John the Baptist prepared the way for Jesus, he gave up his reputation, his time, and his praise for someone else. Is there any way you could demonstrate a similar attitude of giving yourself to someone close to you during this Christmas season?

GOD PREPARED A WOMAN

The coming of the Messiah was promised first to Adam, then to Abraham. Every Jewish woman wondered if she was the one through whom the Messiah would be born. Mary met God's qualifications in both her character and her lineage for giving birth to the Messiah of Israel. Mary's character was as important to God as her ancestry: She was pure, and a virgin. Mary probably never even guessed, however, that she would be God's prepared and chosen woman. Read the account in Luke 1:26-38.

11. How did the angel greet Mary?

12. What was her initial response? How did she feel? (verse 29).

13. How did the angel give Mary confidence in God?

14. What do you think happened in Mary's heart as the angel further explained what God was doing in her body?

15. What was Mary's next response and what did it demonstrate about her relationship to God? (verse 38).

16. Read Mary's song of praise (known as the Magnificat) in Luke 1:46-56.

   a. Summarize what Mary believed about God.

   b. How did Mary's beliefs about God seem to affect the way she responded to the news the angel Gabriel brought her?

17. What can you learn from Mary that can help you face and respond to a difficult situation in your life? How are you able to submit yourself to God's will, care, and faithfulness?

Mary experienced not only exceptional *privilege* but also exceptional *sacrifice.* She joyfully offered to God what was difficult to give: her body, her life, her trust, her future.

GOD PREPARED YOU

According to Ephesians 1:4, we were chosen in Christ before the foundations of the world. Through the sacrifice of His Son, God prepared the way to receive us into His Kingdom.

18. Reflect on your life for a few minutes, focusing on how God used people and circumstances to prepare you to receive His gift of salvation in Jesus Christ. Write down a brief summary of your thoughts. Use it as a prayer of thanksgiving to help you celebrate this Christmas season.

Preparing for Christmas can be a joy as we meditate on how carefully God has prepared Christmas for us. And Christmas can give us hope as we remember 1 Corinthians 2:9-10: "'No eye has seen, no ear has heard, no mind has conceived what God has prepared for those who love him'—but God has revealed it to us by his Spirit."

NEW YEAR'S
New Beginnings

Looking ahead to the routine of another year, many of us long for a new beginning to plan our days wisely, new hope from God's Word to live our lives purposefully.

When we become believers, we become new creatures (2 Corinthians 5:17), with a new heart and a new life. Yet the Christian life is one of *continual* renewal. All renewal begins by seeing ourselves as sinful and in need of God's presence, forgiveness, and healing. Renewal is born within our hearts as we recognize God's greatness and ability to meet all our needs.

Just as water is ever seeking the lowest depths in order to fulfill them, so is Jehovah ever seeking out man's need in order to satisfy it. Where there is need, there is God. Where there is sorrow, misery, unhappiness, suffering, confusion, folly, oppression, there is the I AM, yearning to turn man's sorrow into bliss whenever man will let Him. It is not, therefore, the hungry seeking for bread, but the Bread seeking the hungry; not the sad seeking for joy, but rather Joy seeking the sad; not emptiness seeking fullness, but rather Fullness seeking emptiness. And it is not merely that He supplies our need, but He Himself becomes the fulfillment of our need.

Roy and Revell Hession
(*We Would See Jesus*, Christian Literature Crusade, 1958, page 26)

GOD'S DESIGN FOR NEWNESS

1. a. Read Isaiah 43:18-19. How would you characterize the perspective that God wanted Israel to have?

b. What encouragement might this passage offer as you begin the new year?

2. According to Ezekiel 11:19-20, where does commitment to newness begin?

3. a. What was the new commandment that Jesus gave His disciples in John 13:34?

b. Why do you think Jesus referred to this command as "new"?

c. How might this command become new for you? Write down one practical means by which this passage can make a difference in your new year.

GOD'S DEMONSTRATION OF NEWNESS

After the Church was empowered at Pentecost with a filling of the Holy Spirit, Peter preached a dynamic new message. His listeners were renewed in their spirits. From that point on, their entire lives changed. In Acts 2:37-47 we discover some of the ingredients of their new lives that eventually turned the world upside down for Jesus Christ.

4. What was the crowd's emotional reaction to Peter's message? (Acts 2:37). How did their emotions affect their wills?

33

5. What was the new message? (verse 38).

6. What was the new promise Peter proclaimed (verses 30-33), and for whom was the promise intended?

7. a. How many new converts responded to the message? (verses 41,47).

b. What do you think accounted for this kind of response?

8. What characterized the new believers' fellowship together? (verse 42).

9. How were these new Christians responding to all that was happening in their lives? (verse 43).

10. What do verses 44-46 tell you about their relationship with each other?

11. Look back over your answers to questions 4-10 of this study. Select one characteristic of the new life of the early Church that seems especially significant to you. Based on your reading of the passage (and any other related Scripture verses), what do you think were the key factors that made this new life possible?

The entire book of Acts is filled with examples of newness. Tracing these examples throughout the book would be a fruitful further study.

12. What characteristics of newness would you like to experience in your life and fellowship with others this coming year?

13. What is the basic prerequisite to this newness? (Acts 1:8, Romans 7:6, 8:9-11).

14. Write out a prayer to God expressing your desire for renewal in your heart and life this coming year. You might want to place this prayer in your Bible or in a journal and review it periodically throughout the year.

REFORMATION OR TRANSFORMATION?

If you had won a prize to have your home completely redecorated, how would you feel if the prize amounted to someone coming in and merely rearranging your old furniture? When God promises you a new life, He doesn't mean that He'll just come in and reorganize the "old" you. That would be mere reformation. Instead, God is in the business of *transformation* and *renewal.* His plan is for you to become a new creature.

We can't understand our need for transformation without a deep recognition of the uselessness and deadness of the old self. If we always harbor the feeling that the old self is not all that bad and can somehow be salvaged, we will be looking for reformation instead of transformation. In God's process of renewal, we need to let go of the old in order to grasp the new.

Paul teaches us about this process in Colossians 3:1-17, 22-24. (See also Ephesians 4:22-24.) Read this portion of Paul's letter to the Colossians before answering the following questions.

---

15. In the appropriate columns below, list what we are to put off as we get rid of the old, and what we are to put on as we take on the new.

Put off . . .	Put on . . .

16. In which of the circumstances you just listed do you most often find yourself struggling to put off the old nature?

17. What basic new practice would you like to develop in replacement of your old attitude or behavior?

18. What is the role of the Word of God in making this new practice possible? (verse 16).

19. What basic guidelines in Colossians 3:17 provide for walking in the newness of our life in Christ?

20. a. Can you think of any possible dangers in setting a personal goal for change in order to please someone other than the Lord?

b. Try writing out a prayer to God, based on your study of Colossians 3:1-17, 22-24, in questions 15-19.

Paul says, "We do not lose heart. Though outwardly we are wasting away, yet inwardly we are being renewed day by day" (2 Corinthians 4:16).

Renewal in our hearts leads us to place our lives totally in God's hands so that we are willing to pray this prayer:

"Lord, I am willing to receive what You give.

Lord, I am willing to lack what You withhold.

Lord, I am willing to relinquish what You take.

Lord, I am willing to suffer what You inflict.

Lord, I am willing to be what You require."

VALENTINE'S DAY

Love

Valentine's Day is a time for hearts and flowers, friendship and love. It is a day for expressing love and affection in prose and poetry, for seeking to communicate the sentiments of our hearts. True love proceeds from the heart of God. His love for us reaches the deepest needs in our lives, making us feel significant and secure.

Elizabeth Barrett Browning wrote in a famous love sonnet, "How do I love thee? Let me count the ways." Her expression of emotion echoes the psalmist's praise to God: "Eternal One, my God, richly hast thou worked out thy wondrous purposes for us; there is no one like thee! Were I to tell them, to recount them, they would pass all count" (Psalm 40:5, *Moffatt*).

GOD'S VALENTINE TO US

1. A Valentine message is an expression of love. Read the following passages, and for each one write down how God expresses His love for His people. Envision each one as a message sent to you.

   Isaiah 43:4

Isaiah 62:3

Jeremiah 31:3

Zephaniah 3:17

---

2. What special names of endearment does God use to describe His feelings for those who belong to Him?

Deuteronomy 33:12

Song of Solomon 7:10

Ephesians 5:1-2

Colossians 3:12

3. Paul's prayer for the Ephesians was that they would comprehend more fully the length and breadth and depth and height of God's love, "though it is so great that you will never see the end of it or fully know or understand it" (Ephesians 3:19, TLB). Ephesians 1 is filled with various aspects of God's love for you. As you pray and reflect on His love and what you mean to Him, complete this prayer to Him: "I love You, Lord, because . . . ."

> All our love flows from His heart of love. We are like little pools on the rocks when the great sea washes over them and floods them until they overflow! That is what the love of God does for us. We have no love in ourselves, and our pools would soon be empty if it were not for that great, glorious exhaustless sea of love. My chief prayer is that your pools may be kept full to overflowing.
>
> Amy Carmichael

DEPTH AND DEMONSTRATION OF GOD'S LOVE

4. Read 1 John 4:7-21.

a. How is God's love revealed to us?

b. What characteristic of God's love impresses you the most?

c. If we really live in love, what will characterize our lives?

d. What are some ways for us to love others sacrificially?

---

5. Read in Romans 5:6-10 the condition of those for whom Christ died. Why do you suppose God initiated the relationship?

> It is not that we are loved because we have worth, but that we have worth because we are loved.

---

6. a. What great truth about God's love is communicated in Romans 8:35-39 and Matthew 28:20?

b. Think about some of your greatest insecurities in your relationship with the Lord. How would these Scripture passages affect them if this truth were to really take hold in your life?

---

7. Study the following passages about Jesus' encounters with two sinful women. How did His responses differ from the responses of those around Him?

Luke 7:36-50

He found me with a burden,
And He lifted it from me.
He found me bound and fettered,
And from sin He set me free.
He found me in the darkness,
And He made His light to shine.
Can you wonder that I love Him,
This Savior-Friend divine?

J. Sidlow Baxter
(*Going Deeper*, page 113)

OUR LOVE FOR GOD

8. a. What is the greatest commandment God has given us? (Matthew 22:37-38).

b. Why do you think this commandment is the most important? (Luke 10:38-42).

9. What do Mary's preparations and priorities teach us about her love for Jesus?

> Many people think they are cramming more into their lives . . . when what they are really doing is crowding out those things which most enrich life. Our Lord calls His people away from the merciless, non-stop whirl of the outer world, to quiet, secret, unhurried times with Himself. He has lovely secrets to tell those who wait long enough . . . and often enough in His presence.
>
> J. Sidlow Baxter
> (*Going Deeper*, page 119)

10. a. In John 21:15-17, what questions does Jesus ask Peter? Write out the verse in which each question occurs.

b. Why do you think Jesus repeated His question?

c. What does Jesus' encounter with Peter in this passage suggest about the nature of our love for the Lord?

PRACTICING GOD'S LOVE

11. Look up Luke 22:39-44. Write down everything this passage reveals about Jesus' love for us.

12. a. What do Romans 5:5 and 1 John 4:7-9,13, teach about the source of the love we are to give to God and others?

b. Why is this truth important to our practice of love?

---

13. During the last week of Jesus' life, He communicated to His disciples the most important truths they would need to understand and live by once His physical presence was taken from them. What does Jesus' statement in John 13:34-35 reveal about the power of our witness as believers?

---

14. God's Word is full of instructions on love relationships in families. For example, husbands are instructed to love their wives, and women are told to love their husbands and children (Ephesians 5:25-33, Titus 2:4-5). As you review what love is and what love does, in what ways this week could you send family members or loved ones a living message of your love for them?

49

My prayer for you is that you will overflow more and
more with love for others . . . (Philippians 1:9, TLB).

Love Is . . .
Doing something for others even when you don't
have time.
Love is making others happy when you would
rather be alone,
Not being irritable when others get in your way or
interrupt you.
It is kind and patient regardless of the
circumstances,
Looking for ways to make others happy no matter
who they are.
Love is honest and just, but also tender, under-
standing, and compassionate.
More than a paper valentine or a sentimental love
note,
It is operative all the time—and lasts for a lifetime.
It means not getting upset or angry on the spur of
the moment.
It chooses to be consistent through hard experiences
And finds its joy in God, not in circumstances.

A paraphrase of 1 Corinthians 13:4-8 by Don Highlander
(*The Celebration Book*, Georgia Walker,
ed., Gospel Light, 1977, page 52)

EASTER
The Cross

At the Cross, we see man at his worst and God at His best. We see the deepest sorrow and the greatest love. The message of the Cross has always been charged with emotion. There has never been a time in history when people were not persecuted for preaching the message of the Cross.

When Jesus died on the Cross, His substitutionary suffering for our sins made a permanent difference in the way we come to Him in prayer. The Temple veil being torn in two was a living symbol that we no longer need to make sacrifices or appeal to an intermediary priest. Jesus Christ Himself is our access to God. He is everything we need.

As we study the seven last statements of Jesus on the Cross, we cannot help but love Him more. His words offer us a pattern for praying that can revolutionize our prayer lives.

FORGIVENESS

1. After His Cross was jolted into place, Jesus prayed His first words (Luke 23:34).

   a. What did He pray?

b. What does this prayer reveal about His focus in His life as well as in His death?

> When Jesus forgives us, there will fall from our shoulders the old burden of guilt, and, in its place, will be wrapped around our hearts a radiant sense of warmth, affection, love and acceptance. "You are forgiven. You are mine. You do belong. You are home."
>
> W. Phillip Keller
> (*A Layman Looks at the Lord's Prayer*, Moody Press, 1976, page 116)

---

2. Read Matthew 18:21-35.

a. Describe the difference between the king and his debtor in their reactions to those who owed them money.

b. What debt do we owe for being forgiven? (Matthew 6:14-15).

c. Why is it important for us to forgive others?

d. Is there someone in your life whom you need to forgive? What might be an appropriate response on your part?

SALVATION

3. From a reading of Luke 23:39-43, what impresses you about the two thieves' differing reactions to Jesus?

4. a. What was Jesus' response to the repentant thief?

b. Why do you think Jesus responded that way?

c. How can we be assured that we also will have eternal life? (1 John 5:11-12, John 11:25-26).

---

5. Is there someone in your life to whom you would like to offer the message of salvation? If so, write out Romans 10:1, inserting his or her name.

Think of how you may reach out to this person with a Cross-oriented love, which accepts, forgives, cares, and sacrifices. Salvation is a free gift, but it cost Jesus everything. As we have a part in seeing people born into the Kingdom of God, we will also experience pain and joy.

CARING FOR LOVED ONES

It is difficult to grasp how Jesus Christ, in His weakened, tortured condition, could have the strength and love to reach out to others. He had already prayed for the ones who had tortured

Him, and He had given salvation to the repentant thief. Now, in tenderness, Jesus again ignored His pain and made final arrangements for His mother.

---

6. How did Jesus' death on the Cross explain the prophecy that Mary received from Simeon? (Luke 2:34-35).

---

7. a. What message did Jesus give to Mary in John 19:25-27?

b. What message did He give John?

---

8. What do these statements reveal about Jesus?

9. a. What does Jesus' example here suggest about our behavior toward loved ones?

b. What might be one way in which you could act on His example?

QUESTIONING

For three long hours, Jesus silently endured indescribable agony. Finally, in utter pain and loneliness, He gave vent to His heartbreak.

10. What was Jesus' painful question? (Matthew 27:46).

11. Why did the Father forsake Jesus? (1 Peter 2:24, 2 Corinthians 5:21).

Jesus was forsaken by the Father so that we could enjoy the Father's love for all eternity. He was rejected so that we could be accepted. He was forsaken so that He could promise never to forsake us. Even in this greatest of tragedies, God was in full control, unfolding His purposes. Who would have guessed at the time that the Cross would be God's victory and triumph?

---

12. a. What are some of the situations in your life that you don't understand, for which you are asking God, "Why?"

   b. What encouragement could Romans 8:18 and 8:28 offer you?

During painful times in our lives, God's presence and His promises become our only hope. In the sufferings of the Cross, He has experienced all of our agonies. He invites us to keep coming to Him for comfort, and to keep remembering His love on the Cross.

> *PERFECT TRUST*
> *I may not always know the way*
> *Wherein God leads my feet;*
> *But this I know, that round my path*
> *His love and wisdom meet;*
> *And so I rest content to know*
> *He guides my feet where'er I go.*

I may not always understand
Just why He sends to me
Some bitter grief, some heavy loss,
But, though I cannot see,
I kneel, and whisper through my tears
A prayer for help, and know He hears.

My cherished plans and hopes may fail,
My idols turn to dust,
But this I know, my Father's love
Is always safe to trust;
These things are dear to me, but still
Above them all I love His will.

Oh, precious peace within my heart;
Oh, blessed rest to know
A Father's love keeps constant watch,
Amid life's ebb and flow;
I ask no more than this; I rest
Content, and know His way is best.

Author unknown
(Margaret Wise, *Come for Coffee*,
Moody, 1968, page 78)

THIRSTING

Darkness covered the earth, and God hid His face and His fellowship from Jesus. As Jesus' body was thirsting for water, His spirit was thirsting for the fellowship that He had always known with His Father.

13. Describe the picture that John 19:28-30 provides of Jesus' sufferings on the Cross.

14. In Psalm 42:1-2, how does the psalmist describe his thirsting? What is he looking for to quench his thirst?

> Just as it is normal for the deer to thirst after water brooks, so it is natural for man to thirst after God. He may not know that his thirst is for God, and he will probably try to satisfy that thirst with a substitute that will leave him with more thirst. But a thirst for God is what it is, just the same. God has put Eternity in our hearts, and the temporal cannot satisfy.
>
> Warren Wiersbe
> (*Live Like a King*, Moody Press, 1976, page 82)

15. We thirst because we have a need that must be satisfied. Our lives are filled with needs that will be filled only as we come to Jesus Christ.

   a. If you were able to have a face-to-face encounter with Jesus, what needs in your life would you ask Him to fill?

b. What do Hebrews 2:18 and Hebrews 4:15 tell us about why and how Jesus is able to meet our needs?

COMPLETING THE PURPOSE IN LIFE

16. a. What is the final statement that Jesus made on the Cross, as recorded in John 19:30?

b. How do Jesus' statements in Matthew 20:28 and John 17:1-5 explain what He had finished, that is, His purpose in life?

After Adam and Eve sinned in the Garden of Eden, provision had to be made to atone for sin. The temporary, symbolic solution was the periodic offering of the blood of an unblemished lamb. But on the Cross, Jesus was able to claim victoriously that the complete, *final* solution had been accomplished. There on the Cross He completed the mission for which He had come to earth. He completed the task of doing the whole will of the Father.

Living life purposefully had tremendous rewards for Jesus. It will have meaningful rewards for us as well, as we experience close fellowship with Him.

It is your mission and not your occupation that exalts or degrades you. When the mists have rolled away, we shall see that the scrub woman whose mission it is to exalt Jesus Christ is far more glorified than the princess who is living for self. God is in all of life of which He is the center.

Paul Billheimer
(*Destined for the Cross*, Tyndale House, 1983, page 80)

---

17. What are you doing now that contributes to what you see as your purpose in life?

---

18. a. What major accomplishment would you like to be able to look back on at the end of your life?

b. What does your answer suggest about how you should be living now?

Luke records that when Jesus had completed His mission, He once again prayed to His Father. Having exposed Himself to the hostility of men and the rejection of God, He was ready to die. He knew that His fellowship with the Father would never again be broken.

19. List your observations about Jesus' last words on the Cross, as recorded in Luke 23:46.

It's been said that Jewish parents did not teach their children, "Now I lay me down to sleep," but rather, "Lord, into Your hands I commit my spirit." Hostile hands had nailed Jesus to the Cross; now He was changing hands. The only safe place for us is in the hands of the Lord.

20. Look up Psalm 31:5 and 31:14-15 to find a similar statement of surrender from David. How might you commit yourself to this surrender that is described by David and literally accomplished by Jesus?

The following prayers can provide a helpful way of reviewing your study of the seven last statements of Christ on the Cross. Using this guide, write out your own prayers to God.

Prayer of Forgiveness
Thank the Lord for forgiving you on a regular basis for your lack of trust in Him. Ask Him to continue to forgive you when you fail to have mercy and forgiveness toward others:

Prayer of Salvation
Thank God for your salvation. Ask Him for the ability and opportunities to share His plan of salvation with others:

Prayer of Provision
Thank the Lord for the loved ones He has given you. Ask Him to show you ways of demonstrating love and care for your family:

Prayer of Questioning
Pour out your heart to God for all circumstances in your life that you can't understand:

Ask God for His presence, His promises, and His help in the midst of your disturbing situations:

Prayer of Thirsting
Express to God how you thirst to know Him, how you thirst to have Him meet the deep needs of your heart and the needs of those you love:

Prayer of Life Purpose
Ask God to clarify His purpose for your life:

Ask Him to help you live your life in a focused, purposeful way:

Prayer of Surrender
Surrender everything in your life (for example, your family and your future), as well as your lifestyle itself, into God's hands:

EASTER
The Resurrection

Although Christians have elaborate celebrations at Christmas, perhaps the most joyous of celebrations is Easter. The occasion of Christmas commemorates the beginning of hope: the Incarnation, Jesus' birth, the entrance into the world of the Hope of mankind. His Resurrection is the climax of our hope. It assures us that we serve a living Savior who empowers us to live today and forever with His life flowing through us.

Even in His hours of pain and death on the Cross, Jesus showed us how to live in dependence on God. He knew that the Father was in control. From death, He brought life; from despair, hope. What appeared to be the end was really a new beginning for all who would claim for themselves the reality of Jesus' words: "I am the resurrection and the life. He who believes in me . . . will never die" (John 11:25-26).

THE REALITY OF THE RESURRECTION OF CHRIST

1. Read the Resurrection account in John 20:1-18.

   a. Describe Mary's emotional condition.

b. How was she comforted?

c. What convinced her that Jesus was alive?

d. What was her testimony to the disciples?

2. When Jesus appeared to His disciples, all except Thomas
believed that He had risen from the dead (John 20:19-29).

a. How did Jesus react to Thomas's doubts?

b. What can we learn from Thomas's response to Jesus?

3. Read Paul's declaration in 1 Corinthians 15:4-8. What evidences for the Resurrection does Paul list?

THE RESULT OF THE RESURRECTION OF CHRIST: FORGIVENESS

4. How do we know that Jesus' death was an acceptable and adequate payment to God for our sins? (1 Corinthians 15:17, Romans 4:25).

As long as a person is still in prison, it is assumed that he is still paying for a debt. When a debt is paid in full, the prisoner is released. Thus the release of Jesus from the grip of death dramatically shows us that the debt for our sins has been paid, and it has been paid in full.

5. What did Christ's Resurrection reveal about His power over death? (Acts 2:24, 1 Corinthians 15:25-26, 15:54-55).

In His Resurrection, the Lord crystallized for eternity His identity as the God-man. He continues to carry the marks of His crucifixion on His resurrected body, not as marks of shame, but as marks of triumph and love—as if to remind us for all time that He tasted death in order that we might live forever.

6. a. What effect will death have on the believer? (John 11:25-26, 14:2-3, 2 Corinthians 5:6-8).

b. How should these truths affect our attitude toward death? (Hebrews 2:14-15, 1 John 4:17-18).

70

I'll love Thee in life, I will love Thee in death,
And praise Thee as long as Thou lendest me breath;
And say when the deathdew lies cold on my brow,
"If ever I loved Thee, my Jesus, 'tis now."

William Featherston
(from the hymn, "My Jesus, I Love Thee")

HOPE

7. Read Romans 6:5-10 and Colossians 3:1-3. In the appropriate columns below, list the results of our being united with Christ in His death and in His Resurrection.

Results from His Death	Results From His Resurrection

HIS RESURRECTION LIFE IN US

8. a. What relationship does the believer have with the risen Christ? (Romans 8:9-10, Galatians 2:20, Colossians 1:27).

71

b. What practical difference should this relationship make in the believer's life?

9. a. What is the power available to us? (Ephesians 1:19-20).

b. How can we avail ourselves of this power?

OUR RESPONSE TO THE RESURRECTION

Jesus said, "In this world you will have trouble. But take heart! I have overcome the world" (John 16:33). He proved this fact in His Resurrection. His followers proved it in their lives and deaths.

10. a. How can we also be overcomers? (1 Corinthians 15:57-58, 2 Corinthians 2:14, 1 John 5:4-5).

b. In what areas can we be overcomers? (Romans 12:21, Philippians 4:11-13).

c. In what situations of your life would you like to be an overcomer through the power of Christ's Resurrection?

One of the most dramatic proofs of the Resurrection was the change in the lives of the disciples. After Jesus was crucified, they were discouraged, demoralized, without hope. After Jesus rose from the dead and they saw Him, they began to fearlessly proclaim the Resurrection. After He ascended, they continually preached the truth of the Resurrection and the Lord's indwelling Spirit for those who repented and believed. They lived dynamic lives for the risen Christ as they endured persecution and martyrdom with great joy.

11. Read about the change in Peter's life before and after the Resurrection in Mark 14:66-72 and Acts 4:1-13.

a. List some of the similarities and some of the differences in this before-and-after picture.

73

Before	After

b. How does Peter's transformation indicate the results of the Resurrection that apply to our lives?

---

12. Reflect on Mary's response to the Resurrection: "I have seen the Lord!" (John 20:18). Consider all that you have through Christ living in you, and then write out a prayer of response and thanksgiving to Him.

We thank Thee for the beauty of this day,
for the glorious message that all nature
        proclaims,
the Easter lilies with their waxen throats
eloquently singing the good news,
the birds, so early this morning,
impatient to begin their song;
every flowering tree, shrub, and flaming bush,
a living proclamation from Thee.
Open our hearts that we may hear it too!
Lead us, we pray Thee, to the grave that is empty,
        into the garden of the Resurrection—
where we may meet our risen Lord.
May we never again live as if Thou were dead!
In Thy presence restore our faith, our hope,
        our joy.
Grant to our spirits refreshment, rest and peace.
Maintain within our hearts an unruffled calm,
        an unbroken serenity
that no storms of life shall ever be able to take
        from us.
From this moment, O living Christ,
we ask Thee to go with us wherever we go;
be our Companion in all that we do.
And for this greatest of all gifts,
we offer Thee our sacrifices of thanksgiving.
Amen.

Peter Marshall
(*Hymns for the Family of God*, Paragon Associates, 1976, Selec-
tion 294)

SPRINGTIME
Fruitfulness

After a cold and barren winter, the warm promise of spring is a welcome change. Thoughts of planting and gardening, of bringing forth fruits and flowers, come with the first signs of this joyous season.

The Bible often uses a garden metaphor to speak of spiritual fruitfulness. "The righteous will flourish like a palm tree, they will grow like a cedar in Lebanon; planted in the house of the LORD, they will flourish in the courts of our God. They will still bear fruit in old age, they will stay fresh and green, proclaiming, 'The LORD is upright; he is my Rock' . . ." (Psalm 92:12-14). What a hope of continued fruitfulness throughout our lives!

In Isaiah 27:2-3, God is described as the Gardener who waters, nourishes, carefully tends, and protects us. Can you picture yourself as a plant in the garden of the Lord? What kind of tree would you be? What kind of fruit or flower would you produce? As you ponder this question, consider what the Bible suggests as important ingredients for fruitfulness in our lives.

THE POTENTIAL OF THE SEED

Although seeds look somewhat unimpressive, they hold great potential within them. Who could guess by merely looking at them what they will become? Even the tiny mustard seed can grow into a large bush. And how could anyone foresee the impact a microscopic human embryo might one day have on the world?

---

1. Genesis tells us that when God created the world, He made life forms that would reproduce their own kind—the principle of "like produces like." How does this principle work when a person is born again? (John 1:12-13, 3:6).

---

2. a. What is the unusual quality of the seed (the Word of God) spoken of in 1 Peter 1:23-25?

b. Why is this quality significant?

Some seeds have been known to remain alive for more than a hundred years. The process that eventually breaks down the coat of a seed in the soil is necessary if it is to begin its growth process. Without the eroding factor of the soil and its elements, the seed will remain a seed instead of becoming what it was meant to be. Thus nature demonstrates the principle that life springs forth from death.

3. What does Jesus say about how this principle works in the spiritual realm? (Luke 9:23-25, John 12:24-26).

4. Much of the dying process in our lives is the result of the decisions we make. We "die to ourselves" when we choose the right way, which is harder, rather than the wrong way, which is so much easier. When we do make this difficult choice, the seed of our life grows.

Have you experienced gentle growth as a result of a painful decision you made? Write down what you learned through this experience about the spiritual growth process.

THE NECESSITY OF THE ROOT

The underground root system of a plant is often as extensive as the branch system above the ground. What we can see of a plant is actually only a part of what it is. Before anything grows above ground, the roots must grow, reaching down into the ground. It is a prerequisite for a plant to take root downward before it can bear fruit upward.

Likewise, in our spiritual life, healthy roots will strengthen, stabilize, and feed us.

---

5. In order to become healthy Christians, what kinds of things do we need to be rooted in? (Psalm 1:2-3, Proverbs 12:12, Ephesians 3:17-19, Colossians 2:6-7).

Rooted In	Results

A potted plant will not grow beyond a certain size as long as its roots are restricted. In order to avoid stunting its growth, the plant must be repotted. The plant may wither initially in the new pot, but with proper light and nourishment, it will be healthier and more fruitful as the root system is given freedom of growth.

---

6. Have you recently been "repotted" through a move or a change of seasons in your life? If so, how did you feel initially? What kind of growth have you experienced as a result of the change?

7. What are the symptoms and dangers of not being rooted in Jesus Christ and His Word? (Deuteronomy 29:17-18, Isaiah 5:24, Jeremiah 12:1-2, Hebrews 12:15-16).

8. Contrast the two men and their respective "roots" in Jeremiah 17:5-8.

The man of verses 5-6	The man of verses 7-8

THE PROCESS OF GROWTH

In order to determine if something has life, scientists usually observe it to see if it grows. Growth, then, is a sign or proof of life. Man can only create the environment for growth; he cannot actually cause it.

9. a. According to 1 Corinthians 3:5-7, what is the source of spiritual growth?

b. What implicit warning does Paul provide in this
   passage?

---

10. What will provide the nutrients for our spiritual growth?
    (1 Peter 2:2).

Thy Word is like a garden, Lord,
With flowers bright and fair,
And everyone who seeks may pluck
A lovely cluster there.

Edwin Hodder
(from an old English melody)

---

11. According to Isaiah 58:9-11 and Hosea 6:3, how can we be
    like a "well-watered garden"?

Growth involves more than a mere increase in size. It is not
the purpose of a seed to become a bigger seed. Real growth

82

involves change and development, as in the transformation of a seed to a plant, of an embryo to a man or woman.

12. a. According to 2 Corinthians 3:18, what changes or developments can we expect in our spiritual growth?

   b. In what ways might these changes be noticeable to others?

13. Read Jesus' teaching about the vine and the branches in John 15:1-8.

   a. Write down several observations about this passage. (For example, you might want to respond to the following questions: Who is the gardener? The vine? The branches? What is the role and purpose of the gardener? How are the vine and branches related? What is the purpose of the branches? What are the conditions and results of the branches' relationship to the vine?)

b. What are the most important truths about *abiding* or *remaining* that you discover from your observations?

c. How do John 15:9-10 and 1 John 2:5-6 help explain what it means to abide or remain in Jesus?

Our blessed Lord desires to call us away from ourselves and our own strength, to Himself and His strength. Let us accept the warning and turn with great fear and self distrust to Him to do His work. "Our life is hid with Christ in God." That life is a heavenly mystery, hid from the wise among Christians and revealed unto babes. The childlike spirit learns that life is given from Heaven every day and every moment to the soul that accepts its teaching and seeks its all in the Vine. Abiding in the True Vine then comes to be nothing more than the restful surrender of the soul to let Christ have all and work all, as completely in nature the branch knows and seeks nothing but the Vine.

Andrew Murray
(*The True Vine*)

THE PURPOSEFULNESS OF FRUIT

Once Jesus cursed a fig tree that had no fruit for Him. As a result, it withered instantly (Matthew 21:19). How much more barren is the believer without spiritual fruit! Jesus said that as a result of our abiding we will bring forth much fruit. In fact, He said that we have been chosen to bear fruit that will remain (John 15:16). Fruit is delicious, colorful, and fragrant. Spiritual fruit brings joy to the Gardener.

14. What is the purpose of fruit in a believer's life? (Luke 6:43-49, John 15:8).

> Our Father, Thou comest seeking fruit. Teach us, we pray Thee, to realize how truly this is the one object of our existence, and of our union to Christ. Make it the one desire of our hearts to be branches, so filled with the Spirit of the Vine, as to bring forth fruit abundantly.
>
> Andrew Murray
> (*The True Vine*)

15. a. What are some kinds of spiritual fruit produced in the believer? (Galatians 5:22-23, 2 Peter 1:5-8).

85

b. How does this fruit bring glory to the Gardener?

16. What kind of influence can we have in helping fruit to grow in others' lives? (Proverbs 11:30, Romans 1:13).

17. Contrast the two types of "harvesting" in the following passages:

Sowing	Reaping
Hosea 10:12-13	
Matthew 13:23, 37-43	
Galatians 6:7-10	

18. Picture yourself today as a seedling in the garden court of God. What do you need in order to grow into a fruitful plant?

Has the seed of salvation been planted in your heart? Are your roots growing deep in His love and His Word? Are you abiding in Jesus Christ and trusting Him for spiritual growth? Are you asking God to make you fruitful for His glory? As you grow in Him, you can expect to receive a bouquet of God's blessings and become a fragrant aroma of Jesus Christ to those around you.

God, who gives seed to the farmer to plant, and later on, good crops to harvest and eat, will give you more and more seed to plant and will make it grow so that you can give away more and more fruit from your harvest.

Yes, God will give you much so that you can give away much, and when we take your gifts to those who need them they will break out into thanksgiving and praise to God for your help.

2 Corinthians 9:10-11
(TLB)

IDEAS FOR
HOLIDAY
ACTIVITIES

IDEAS FOR HOLIDAY ACTIVITIES | INTRODUCTION

Holidays can become significant events when we capitalize on them to teach spiritual truths. Even secular holidays can help introduce a rhythm of biblical purpose into our lives and those of our families.

For small group Bible studies, holiday seasons offer opportunities to break from a habitual routine and agenda. Focusing together on a great biblical event or a significant aspect of God's grace in our lives can breathe a fresh air of fellowship into a familiar gathering of believers.

Seasonal celebrations also offer us the chance to reach out as individuals and families to those around us in a natural way. Holidays create festive occasions for inviting others into our homes, for the purpose of introducing them to Jesus Christ or for encouraging them in their lives.

The ideas on the following pages can be used in addition to the Bible studies in this booklet, or in place of them. Pick and choose among them for whatever best suits your needs or those of the small group you may be a part of. The New Year, Easter, and Springtime ideas are intended for Christians who are already involved in a small group study. The Thanksgiving, Christmas, and Valentine's Day suggestions can be extended to include nonChristians as well, by creating an atmosphere where they might experience the fragrance of Jesus Christ as they are exposed to reflection on spiritual truths.

THANKSGIVING

A get-together over brunch can be an easy and relaxed way for you to enjoy the celebration of Thanksgiving with others. You might find it works well to hold a brunch immediately following a special session of your group, using the Thanksgiving Bible study on pages 9-20. You might just want to hold the brunch separately from your group's study sessions as a special time of fellowship, using the ideas listed here in place of the Bible study if the people in your group are especially busy with personal preparations. And why not consider inviting a couple of nonChristian friends? This could be an ideal time to expose them to Christians in a warm, non-threatening atmosphere.

The week before you meet for the brunch, ask your group members to do three things (consider also adapting these ideas for families in preparation for Thanksgiving Day):

1. Write out an acrostic, using the word "Thanksgiving," to itemize a list of things for which you're thankful. You could also use the letters to suggest words for composing a prayer of thanks. All you need is a heart overflowing with thanks to God, not necessarily cleverness or creativity. (Use the example on pages 96-97 to help those who are unfamiliar with this kind of writing exercise.)

2. Read Psalms 103 and 145. Make a list of all that God has given us, according to these Psalms.

3. Write two short letters to family members or loved

ones—to be opened Thanksgiving morning—telling them what in their lives you are thankful for.

Also ask each woman in the group to bring a platter of goodies with a harvest theme (for example, pumpkin or zucchini bread, homemade apple butter, cinnamon-apple coffee cake, a mound of grapes with cheese wedges, or spiced tea).

CREATING THE ATMOSPHERE

To fill your home with a lovely holiday scent, boil some cloves in water as your friends are arriving. (Don't let all the water evaporate, or you will have another scent!)

Setting the table: Use an orange or brown tablecloth, or placemats, with the alternate color napkins and candles. Try creating a centerpiece with an autumn theme.

Placecards: Write a 2-line poem for each person:

We loved hearing how Jesus came into her life
and changed her ways of being a wife.

She loves to sing, her cooking's great,
with five kids, she has an excuse for being late.

Have the people find their placecards and stand behind their seats, until everybody has found one. The poems may be very amateur, but everyone enjoys them and has to read his or hers aloud before sitting down. Each person has this little memento to take home.

Beside each person's plate, place a real leaf (which you have pressed ahead of time, or an artificial leaf cut from construction paper). On that leaf, place five kernels of corn. After everyone has been seated and the blessing has been said, draw everyone's attention to the five kernels of corn and have someone read the following account:

Five Grains of Corn

THANKSGIVING is distinctly an American holiday. There is nothing like it anywhere else in the world. It celebrates neither a savage battle nor the fall of a great city. It does not mark the anniversary of a great conqueror or the birthday of a famous statesman. The American Thanksgiving Day is the expression of a deep feeling of gratitude by our people for the rich productivity of the land, a memorial of the dangers and hardships through which we have safely passed, and a fitting recognition of all that God in His goodness has bestowed upon us.

In early New England, it was the custom at Thanksgiving time to place five kernels of corn at every plate as a reminder of those stern days in the first winter when the food of the Pilgrims was so depleted that only five kernels of corn were rationed to each individual at a time. The Pilgrim Fathers wanted their children to remember the sacrifice, sufferings, and hardships through which they had safely passed—a fitting hardship that made possible the settlement of a free people in a free land. They wanted to keep alive the memory of that sixty-three-day trip taken in the tiny Mayflower. They desired to keep alive the thought of that stern and rockbound coast, its inhospitable welcome, and the first terrible winter, which took such a toll of lives. They did not want their descendants to forget that on the day in which their ration was reduced to five kernels of corn, only seven healthy colonists remained to nurse the sick, and nearly half their members lay in the windswept graveyard on the hill. They did not want to forget that when the Mayflower sailed back to England in the spring, only the sailors were aboard.

The use of five kernels of corn placed by each plate was a fitting reminder of a heroic past. Symbolically, it may still serve as a useful means of recalling those great gifts for which we are grateful to God.

Bliss Forbush

People in general enjoy quizzes, so before they share their acrostics, try quizzing them on Thanksgiving history. Here are some questions:

Who were the Pilgrims?

What were the conditions in England at the time they left their country?

How many Pilgrims left for the new land?

How long did the journey take?

What was the trip like?

Where did they land?

What happened that first year?

How did the Indians help the Pilgrims?

How did they express their thanks to the Indians?

Conclude your time together by going around the table allowing each person to share his or her acrostic and anything else of a thanksgiving nature to share with the others (perhaps some insights from reading Psalms 103 and 145).

Close with a time of group prayer, thanking God for your time together. Encourage the group members to try some of the brunch activities in their own families on Thanksgiving Day.

SAMPLE ACROSTIC

My Thanksgiving List: "Intangibles"

Thankfulness: God convinced me several years ago that He could begin turning a marriage around if one person was thankful instead of critical. I'm so thankful He showed me the power of *thankfulness.*

Hungering after Christ and His goodness that He placed in me until I had to get into His Word.

Accountability: He's given me Christian friends who will know me and hold me accountable for doing what He challenges me to do.

Needs: My needs are being met by God or being used by Him to change me.

Knowledge of Him that He allows me to have, and knowledge of His working in others' hearts.

Sheep that stray and are drawn back to the Good Shepherd. Thank you, Lord!

96

Guilt: My guilt has been taken away by Jesus' blood. I appreciate the joy and freedom of forgiveness because I no longer experience the bondage of guilt.

Infirmities that are used to teach me about His upholding power, allowing me to experience His strength through my weakness.

Victories that I realized I was incapable of!

Interceding that is done on my behalf by friends and by the very Spirit of God.

Nothing can separate me from the love of God—"Neither death nor life, neither angels nor demons, neither the present nor the future, nor any powers, neither height nor depth, nor anything else in all creation" (Romans 8:38-39).

Good work that God has begun in me and has promised to perfect.

Linda Sebatke

IDEAS FOR HOLIDAY ACTIVITIES | CHRISTMAS

Many groups take a break from meeting together for several weeks around Christmas time. You might want to spend one special session together, centered around your discoveries from the Bible study on pages 21-29. Singing some Christmas carols together will add to your fellowship.

If you choose not to have a group session with the Bible study, consider a social evening over coffee and Christmas cookies. Invite some nonChristian friends. Most people are especially open to spiritual inspiration this time of year. They ache to find Christ in Christmas, but they don't know how. This "Christmas coffee" can be a great forum for communicating the life-changing message of the gospel as people are drawn into the festive atmosphere of a home for a time of spiritual sharing.

IDEAS FOR A "CHRISTMAS COFFEE"

If your group is small enough, a cozy way to share your time together is around the kitchen or dining room table. Place a small candle by each person's plate to create a festive atmosphere, and emphasize that Christmas is a special time of remembering that Jesus is "the light of the world." Ask each woman in the group to bring her favorite Christmas cookies, along with the recipe. Divide the leftovers among all of you, or take them to the home of one of the people in your group who is not feeling well or needs special encouragement.

Have the people in your group come prepared with one or two of the following ideas:

1. Describe a favorite Christmas tradition—something you always did in your family when you were growing up, or something you are doing now in your family.

2. Bring a favorite Christmas story, poem, or work of art— or the background information on your favorite Christmas carol.

3. Choose your favorite character(s) in the Christmas story—the shepherds, the angels, Simeon, Anna, Mary, Joseph, Elizabeth, etc.— and discuss the reasons for your choice. (Ask someone who reads well to read Luke 2 aloud to refresh everyone's memory.) NonChristians are usually open to hear the Christmas story and get refreshed on the facts. They might really enjoy the opportunity to share their reasons for favoring a particular character.

When you sit down together, spend some time sharing the reflections each of you has brought from the ideas listed above. This will probably take a while—but if you have time, you might want to look at a few Scripture passages together. In advance of your get-together, pick out key Scripture passages that tell of something God has given us. Write them on strips of paper and put them into a basket to be passed around the table. Ask each person to read his or her passage aloud. Then use this question for discussion: "How should we respond in appreciation to these gifts from the Lord?"

After your sharing time, have each person in your group draw the name of someone else in the Bible study. Tell the group that the most meaningful gift we could possibly give is an intangible one—a gift of time, a labor of love. Have each person share one intangible gift he or she can give this Christmas time to the person whose name is on the slip of paper. Examples: "I would like to give you an hour of praying together once a month," or "I would like to babysit for you three mornings so that you can have some time alone," or "I would like to give you a wish and a prayer that these last few months at home with your daughter before she goes to college will be very meaningful," or "I'd like to invite your whole family over for lunch after church some Sunday."

Close your time together by reading excerpts from "If Jesus Had Not Come," the following Christmas poem by Paul Rees. Pray together, perhaps about how Jesus has made a difference this past year or what life would be like without Him. Consider singing a carol or two before ending your evening.

"If I had not come..."
That's the way Jesus began one of His sentences. The haunting suggestiveness of it is overpowering. The smug complacency with which I have come to take Christmas for granted is suddenly seized and shattered. Gone in a trice, a million cheery lights and merry laughs.
Suppose Christ had not come. Suppose there had been...

> *no manger birth*
> *no star in the east*
> *no angel rhapsody*
> *no awe-struck shepherds*
> *no Sermon on the Mount*
> *no Healer of hurts and hearts*
> *no reconciling Cross*
> *no empty tomb*
> *no empowering Spirit*
> *no community of the caring....*

If Jesus had not come, our thinking about God would have gone along gropingly, forever faltering, forever fractured. For is it not Jesus who, practically as well as conceptually, invests God with love, the universe with meaning, and life with immeasurably glorious possibilities?
If Jesus had not come! What mind can compass the immensity of the gap, the vastness of the void, that would have been created in the human story?

> *History without its fairest Figure*
> *Literature without its sublimest passages*
> *Music without its richest compositions*
> *Eloquence without its loftiest flights*
> *Philosophy without its most luminous insights*
> *Theology without its Christology*
> *Servanthood for others without its model and motive*

Sin without a Conqueror
The world without a Redeemer
Death without a Destroyer
Heaven without assurance or allure . . . .
Ah! But I remember another word of His . . .
"I am come!"
My word, what a difference!
He has come . . .
to Mary's encircling arms
to the shepherds' wondering gaze
to Jerusalem's pools and pathways
to Galilee's hills and shores
to the classy rich and cashless poor
to the arrogant, the ignorant, the errant
to the resolute, the dissolute, the prostitute.
There has never been a coming like it. (Yes, there will be
another, but even it will not be like this one.)
More than an effort, it was an effect.
More than attempt, it was an act.
More than a desire, it was a deed.
To reveal, to suffer, to die, to live again.
To enlighten our darkness, to liberate us from our
chains, to save us from ourselves, to bring us to God and to
mankind and to heaven.
That's why He came! That's why He is here!

Paul Rees

IDEAS FOR HOLIDAY ACTIVITIES NEW YEAR'S

After the excitement and fatigue of the Christmas season, most of us desire a return to a regular rhythm of life, with God's perspective on our priorities.

Within the first week of the new year, invite members of your group to a special morning session devoted to reflection and preparation for entering this brand new year. Emphasize that this "new beginnings" session is optional, and will focus on time alone with God. Ask those who want to come to bring a Bible, a notebook, and an expectant heart.

When you assemble, spend the first half hour together— praying that God will use your time, singing a few devotional songs or hymns, and discussing instructions for the time alone with God.

TIME ALONE WITH GOD

Give each person a cup of coffee or tea, a candle in a little holder, and a place at a table or desk in a corner of a room. Adapt the following schedule to fit the needs of your particular group.

9:00-10:30 Fellowship with God.
    Prayer: "Lord, show me wonderful things about You from Your Word and open up my ears to hear what You are saying to me."

Read from Psalms 121-150. As you read, keep a list, according to these three categories:

Lord, I love You because You are . . .	Things I want You to do in and through my life	Prayer ideas for others

10:30-11:00 Make a Worry List.

1. Give some thought to current conflicts, problems, concerns, or frustrations. List anything that is bothering you. Number each of these items. No matter how small an item is, if it is of concern to you, list it. Ask God to reveal to you anything else that is a point of concern.
2. Every worry that is currently eating at you should be on that piece of paper. When you are satisfied that all of your concerns have been listed, go on to step 3.
3. Go through the list item by item. For each one, note whether you can or can't do something about your concern (it might be beyond your control). If there is nothing you can do about a given item, then spend some time in prayer about it. If you feel you *can* take action on a particular item, you should also pray about it, but then make a "do list" of specific things you would like to do to help resolve it.

After you have gone through many of these concerns, you will have several items on a "do list." Number these items according to priority.

11:00-11:45 Write out prayers for your family and friends, and about your responsibilities.

11:45-12:00 Thank God for your time with Him!

At the conclusion of your time, each person could share one aspect of who God is and why that moves him or her to a response of love for Him.

| IDEAS FOR HOLIDAY ACTIVITIES |
VALENTINE'S DAY

Valentine's Day is a sentimental observance marked by hearts and flowers, but it is also a natural time for discussing friendship and love.

Your group may choose to do the Valentine's Day Bible study on love (pages 41-50), or you might want to get together for an informal party using the suggestions listed below as the focus for your interchange. A Valentine's Day get-together provides an excellent opportunity for including nonChristians who seem to be interested in spiritual things.

IDEAS FOR A VALENTINE'S DAY GET-TOGETHER

You might make it your prayer that everyone in your group would feel loved by God and each other. It's been said that "you're nobody until somebody loves you!" What an accomplishment it would be if each person left knowing that he or she was *somebody!*

Refreshments brighten up any occasion and provide an ideal icebreaker. Consider serving heart-shaped scones with strawberry jam and whipped cream, or any cookies or cake in the shape of a heart.

If there is a woman in your group with an artistic flair, she might create a large heart-shaped valentine with poster board and lace and the words of Jeremiah 31:3 inscribed in the center: "I have loved you with an everlasting love; I have drawn you with loving-kindness." Hang this piece in a central place as a decoration, or use it as a centerpiece, and explain to the group members that it is God's message of love to each of them.

Ask each person to bring something that reminds him or her of love—a letter, a gift, a special memory, a song, a book, or poem. Take turns presenting each memento to the group.

If you want to spend more time together of a reflective nature, consider using one or two of the following questions (choose the ones you feel will most naturally encourage sharing in your group):

1. Can you remember the first valentine you ever received, or any valentine that was especially important to you?

2. Have you ever heard a legend about Valentine's Day? (You might want to read the following poem by Helen Steiner Rice, which describes one such legend.)

THE LEGEND OF THE VALENTINE
The legend says St. Valentine
Was in a prison cell
Thinking of his little flock
He had always loved so well
And, wanting to assure them
Of his friendship and his love
He picked a bunch of violets
And sent them by a dove . . .
And on the violets' velvet leaves
He pierced these lines divine
That simply said, "I LOVE YOU
AND I'M YOUR VALENTINE" . . .
So through the years that followed
From that day unto this,
Folks still send messages of love
And seal them with a kiss . . .
Because a saint in prison
Reached through prison bars one day
And picked a bunch of violets
And sent them out to say
That faith and love can triumph

No matter where you are
For faith and love are greater
Than the strongest prison bar.

Helen Steiner Rice

3. Someone identified three basic kinds of love: *if* love (I will love you if you meet certain requirements: if you are good to me, if you meet my needs, etc.); *because* love (I love you because of something you are, something you have, something you do, because of how you make me feel); and *in spite of* love, or *unconditional* love (love with no strings attached, which expects nothing in return, which is not deserved).

4. Think of a good friend you have or have had. What qualities of that person come to mind? How did that person make you feel loved?

5. Have you ever had an experience in which you knew God's love in a meaningful way?

6. Did any person's love play a major role in your becoming a Christian?

7. Has it been because of someone's love and care that you have been able to experience growth in your Christian life?

A closing time of praying together can focus on thankfulness for God's love and our desire to become channels of His love to others.

Consider sending a personalized valentine home with each person. You could make them by using some of the Scripture passages from the Bible study on pages 41-50, writing in each person's name. That way each person will have a loving remembrance of your time together, as well as some specific Scripture passages to dwell on (and possibly memorize).

IDEAS FOR
HOLIDAY
ACTIVITIES **EASTER**

GROUP IDEA FOR THE CROSS STUDY

The Bible study on the Cross (pages 51-65) leads into a personal prayer based on Jesus' last words on the Cross.

If your group chooses to use the Cross study, ask each member to bring his or her written prayer to your meeting. After sharing your discoveries from the study, break your group up into smaller clusters (of 2, 3, or 4 each), and let each person read aloud his or her prayer. This manner of group prayer can be especially helpful for those people who have difficulty praying out loud in a group. Afterward, discuss your reactions to writing out a prayer, and the ways in which this kind of praying could make a difference in your individual prayer lives or even in your group prayer time.

GROUP IDEAS FOR THE RESURRECTION STUDY

If your group chooses to do the Bible study on the Resurrection (pages 67-75), consider adding to your discussion a time for sharing reflections on the significance of this tremendous event to each of you personally.

Before you meet to go through the Bible study together, invite several people from your group (or those who express the desire) to prepare a three-to-five-minute testimony on "What Easter Means to Me" (use the sample on pages 110-111 if you'd like an example to stimulate thinking about what kinds of things to include). Encourage each volunteer to dwell on meaningful applications from the Bible and practical ways in which Jesus Christ has made a difference in his or her life. Writing out the testimony beforehand, and even discussing it with the group leader, might help those who have little experience in speaking before a group.

Structure your time together in whatever way will best meet the needs of your group. You could ask those people who are reading their testimonies to do so before or after the Bible study. Your group might decide not to do the Bible study at all, and instead just use the testimonies as a springboard for a special time of fellowship. Be sensitive to what will work best for the individuals in your group, and tailor your activities together accordingly.

After your sharing of the Bible study and/or testimonies, consider asking each member to complete one of the following sentences:

1. Because of what Jesus Christ has done for me, I want to *be* more. . . .

2. Because of what Jesus Christ has done for me, I want to *do* more. . . .

You'll probably end up with a variety of answers, which can help stimulate all of you to fresh ways of following Jesus—a wonderful outcome for your focus on Easter. A nice way to close your meeting is with prayer, having each person pray for the person on the right-hand side that God would enable him or her to accomplish new things for Him. Read aloud Proverbs 13:19: "A longing fulfilled is sweet to the soul."

SAMPLE TESTIMONY: "What Easter Means to Me"
When I was asked to share my thoughts on what Easter means to me, a kaleidoscope of words whirled through my mind: forgiveness . . . joy . . . hope . . . new life . . . meaning . . . giving. And I reminisced over our unforgettable two days at the Oberammergau Passion Play in Germany this past springtime, where the live presentation of the Passion Week made the Bible events even more vivid to me. Interestingly, the Passion Play doesn't open with the manger scene or with Christ's miracles or with the procession of palms. It opens in a garden. The narrator describes the opening tableau of Adam and Eve

being banished from the Garden of Eden, and then he goes on to explain that without the backdrop of this tableau, there would be no need for Jesus, for His death on the Cross, for the Resurrection . . . for Easter.

God chose man as a creature to love and obey Him. Man chose to go his own way. As a result, the original fellowship that God and man had together was broken. One reason that Easter means so much to me is that I could see myself in that tableau of choosing my own way. My university days were filled with struggles against God. A sense of having tarnished my own life made me desire so much an inner peace with Him. Although I was deeply aware of my need for forgiveness, I continued vacillating between going God's way and going my own way.

But one day the magnet of the message of the Cross—that Jesus gave His life so that I could be forgiven and have a personal relationship with God—became the strongest pull in my life, and I made a commitment of my life to Jesus Christ. How thankful I am for the Cross and for the forgiveness that flooded my heart on that day, and for the many times I've continued to go to Jesus for forgiveness. Easter means God doing something for me that I couldn't do for myself.

The Cross and the Resurrection give my life meaning. In these days of rootlessness, we have a message to pass on to our children that is changeless and real. It is not pie-in-the-sky-by-and-by. It is a meaningful relationship with God, a message of forgiveness, of the security of knowing that God is in control of our lives. The outworking of that message is that since God gave His Son and Jesus gave His life, it is immensely important that we give ourselves to our family and to others. The Resurrection message says that Jesus Christ is alive, and that because of all that He experienced for us, He will give us the strength we need to give and to love.

Jesus said to her, "I am the resurrection and the life. He who believes in me will live, even though he dies; and whoever lives and believes in me will never die."

John 11:25-26

SPRING LUNCHEON IDEAS

The Springtime study on fruitfulness is intended for the end of your Bible study year—a good time to prepare people's hearts for the coming summer. The change to a busy yet unstructured season can leave us feeling adrift and unfocused, cluttering up the garden of our hearts. This turning point provides an excellent opportunity for focusing our attention on God's purpose for our lives: to bear fruit for Him.

An enjoyable way to emphasize this theme of fruitfulness is by holding a spring luncheon, which lends itself easily to a garden theme. The table can be decorated with fresh lilacs or other flowers from someone's back yard. Before the luncheon, ask each person to bring one illustration from his or her gardening experiences—either a failure or a success. Sharing these experiences can help all of you get into the gardening mood and provide an icebreaker for your time together.

You might also ask each person to bring a favorite gardening principle or verse from the Bible that is currently relevant to his or her life. Taking turns explaining these insights can deepen relationships and focus the discussion around the Word and God's work in the lives of your group members.

Another idea for a discussion springboard is to read gardening illustrations aloud from the works of Christian writers. Five are reprinted here for your convenience; choose from among them, or make your own selections, if you wish. After

reading an illustration to your group, try asking either of the
following questions:

1. In gardening, man does his part, but the results are
God's part as the Creator and Sustainer of our natural world.
Both aspects are important. What do you think is the most
important factor in keeping the garden of your life beautiful?

2. Cultivation of our inner garden happens through
spending time alone with God in prayer and reading His
Word. In the busyness of your summer, when and how will you
spend these precious moments?

GORDON MACDONALD: DISCIPLINE IN OUR INNER GARDEN

"For me the appropriate metaphor for the inner spiritual center is a garden, a place of potential peace and tranquility. This
garden is a place where the Spirit of God comes to make self-
disclosure, to share wisdom, to give affirmation or rebuke, to
provide encouragement, and to give direction and guidance.
When this garden is in proper order, it is a quiet place, and
there is an absence of busyness, of defiling noise, of confusion.

"The inner garden is a delicate place, and if not properly
maintained it will be quickly overrun by intrusive under-
growth. God does not often walk in disordered gardens. And
that is why inner gardens that are ignored are said to be
empty.

"That is exactly what Howard Rutledge was struggling with
when the pressure was at its highest in 'Heartbreak' prison [a
POW prison in North Vietnam]. Total isolation, frequent beat-
ings, and deteriorating health had made his world a hostile
place. What resources did he have to draw upon that would
sustain him? According to his own admission he'd squandered
opportunities earlier in life to store up strength and resolve in
his inner garden. 'I was too busy, too preoccupied,' he says, 'to
spend one or two short hours a week thinking about the really
important things.' Nevertheless, what little he had from his
childhood, he seized and developed. Suddenly, God was a very
real and very important part of his existence.

"Bringing order to the spiritual dimension of our private
worlds is spiritual gardening. It is the careful cultivation of

spiritual ground. The gardener turns up soil, pulls out unwanted growth, plans the use of the ground, plants seeds, waters and nourishes, and enjoys the harvests that result. All of this is what many have called spiritual discipline.

"I love the words of Brother Lawrence, a reflective Christian of many centuries ago who used the metaphor of a chapel:

"'It is not needful always to be in church to be with God. We make a chapel of our heart, to which we can from time to time withdraw to have gentle, humble, loving communion with Him. Everyone is able to have these familiar conversations with God. Some more, some less—He knows our capabilities. Let us make a start. Perhaps He only waits for us to make one whole-hearted resolve. Courage! We have but a short time to live.'

"Let us begin soon, Brother Lawrence coaxes us; time is short! The discipline of the spirit must begin *now*."

Gordon MacDonald
(Ordering Your Private World, Moody Press, 1984, pages 128-129)

W. PHILLIP KELLER:
THE WORD OF GOD PRODUCES GOOD SOIL

"This is what God, the Great, Good Gardener has to do in our lives. We are not naturally 'good ground.' Beyond our hardness and perverseness He sees the potential locked up in our stony souls. He works on us in hope and love.

"None of us is too tough for Him to tackle. In spite of our perverseness, pride, and pollution He can transform us from a wasteland to a well-watered garden. We should want it that way. It does not come easily. It does not happen in a single day. The digging, the clearing, the cultivation may seem to us to be devastating; the disciplining of our souls may seem severe. Yet afterwards it produces the peaceable fruits of His own planting (see Hebrews 12:10-11).

"Too many of us as Christians are content to remain wild, waste land. We much prefer to stay untouched by God's good hand. In fact we are frightened of having our little lives turned over by the deep work of His convicting Spirit. We don't want the shearing, cutting, powerful thrust of His Word to lay us

115

open to the sunlight of His own presence. We prefer to remain weedy ground and stony soil—or pathetic pathway people.

"We delude ourselves into thinking that out of our old unchanged characters and dispositions somehow a good crop is coming forth. It simply cannot be. You simply do not gather grapes from a thistle patch nor figs from wild brambles. And the good gardener does not even come there looking for fruit. It is strictly a no-crop condition. It is a total loss to both ourselves and God.

"Our Lord was very specific in describing the spiritual aspects of productive people:

"(1) They are people who bear His Word and all that it implies.

"(2) They are people who receive and accept that Word.

"(3) They are people whose lives because of that Word produce the fruit of God's Gracious Spirit in their characters, conduct, and conversation."

W. Phillip Keller
(*Four Types of Soil*, Pickering Inglis, 1979, pages 66-67)

EDITH SCHAEFFER: THE GARDEN OF OUR FAMILY LIFE

"Have you exclaimed over gorgeous English gardens with their clipped lawns, precise flower beds, sunken pools with water lilies? And have you found that the family couldn't afford a gardener, so that the father or mother of the household got up before everyone else—to plant and keep the garden in this state? Somebody has to get up early, stay up late, do *more* than the others, if the human garden is to be a thing of beauty.

"No person is perfect. The one doing much for the sake of the others can explode suddenly, and spoil a whole patch of time and results! No results are perfect. The work can suddenly seem to be of no avail. Why bother? It is worth fighting for, the environment that is slowly disappearing, since it produces lasting human families which produce more stable, balanced human beings."

Edith Schaeffer
(*What Is a Family?*, Fleming H. Revell, 1975, page 45)

"At times Fran's anger causes him to feel like throwing something. There was an ivy plant which came over from Champéry to Huémoz with us when we moved, and became the main plant on the coffee table. When a flare of temper would strike Fran like a cyclone, he'd lift up this red clay pot and heave the ivy on the floor. The floor was linoleum and the only damage done would be a scattered pile of dark brown earth mixed with bits of the clay-red pottery, and an ivy with its roots exposed lying somewhere on the floor. A broom, dustpan and brush, another pot brought up out of the woodshed, some extra dirt added to the old, maybe a shot of fertilizer, a pail of hot sudsy water and a cloth—and the room would be cleaner than before, the ivy repotted and back in its place! . . .

"Yes, the ivy was thrown a number of times, but then the day arrived when it graduated to a lovely bracket on the wall. It had grown far too many long fronds to stay on the table, and Fran carefully put it up with pins to climb along the wall. Never has it been thrown since! . . . That ivy says a number of things silently with its variety of sizes and shades of green leaves spreading, flourishing, and continuing to be a thing of beauty. It says that it didn't die from being thrown, because the repotting took place so quickly, water wasn't forgotten, and loving care was given the rest of the time. It demonstrates something of the whole family, generation added to generation, as the leaves are added to the plant. The ivy has grown, so the family has grown. . . .

"It also demonstrates the fact that perfection which is held up as an ideal can be destructive. One needs to resolve, 'I am going to do better; I won't do that kind of thing,' and one needs to know that changes and discoveries of how to avoid flare-ups can help a new family not to repeat the old mistakes. But such a thing as that 'ivy masterpiece' in the museum of memories can be a tremendous safeguard. When some new little family is frightened of the emotions of anger, disappointment, disgust, or dismay because of what one or the other has done, the remembrance of the ivy can remind both the calm one and the upset one, 'This doesn't need to be the end; just think how many times the ivy was thrown, and how many times it all got cleaned up and repotted. Our human

117

relationship can continue to get better and stronger just as the plant continued to grow with a sturdy, healthy growth.' There can be a 'repotting and watering' of a human relationship, too."

Edith Schaeffer
(*What Is a Family?*, pages 203-205)

ALLEGRA MCBIRNEY: PRUNING AND THE PRIORITIES OF OUR LIVES

"Lord, I got this booklet, GUIDE TO PRUNING,
Supposedly to learn about my plants;
But it turns out that I have learned far more about
You as the Vine, me as a branch, the Father as the Gardener
Than I have learned about my garden's care!

"I've seen that all these testings lately
And the tears that I've been through
Have really been the pruning knife and not the rod.
My GUIDE TO PRUNING says that 'cutting back
Will head off growth in wrong directions.'
Now I see that through these trials
You've done exactly that!
There were some wrong directions, weren't there, Lord?

"It also says,
'Good pruning cuts the shoots that sap the strength.'
And surely my distractions sapped me of the strength
And time—and love—that should have gone to You!
I needed Your professional attention!

"You know, I used to think that all this 'cutting back'
Was wrecking me
But now I see that it has 'forced new growth!'
You knew it would!
Now make me bear much more—and sweeter—fruit . . .

"I see at last Your purpose in my tears:
Your pruning was to bring my branch perfection,
Not destruction.

118

Your GUIDE TO PRUNING is Your Love . . . .

"The cutting back was painful, and yet through it all
I felt Your closeness in a very special way;
And now I know the Gardener is never quite so near
The branch as when with His own hand
He's pruning it . . . ."

Allegra McBirney
(Interest magazine, June 1976, pages 48-49)

TERESA OF AVILA:
THE GARDEN OF OUR PRAYER LIFE

"A beginner in prayer must look upon himself as making a garden. There our Lord may take His delight, but in a soil that is unfruitful and full of weeds. His Majesty roots up the weeds to replace them with good plants. Let us take for granted that this is already done when a soul is determined to give itself to prayer and has begun the practice of it.

"As good gardeners, we have by the help of God to see that the plants grow. We should water them carefully so that they will not die, but rather produce blossoms. These will send forth much fragrance which is so refreshing to our Lord that He may come often for His delight into this garden and take pleasure Himself in the midst of these virtues."

Teresa of Avila
(A Life of Prayer, Multnomah Press, 1983, pages 75-76)

BIBLE STUDY MATERIALS
FROM NAVPRESS

BIBLE STUDY SERIES

DESIGN FOR DISCIPLESHIP—seven books and leader's guide
EXPERIENCING GOD—three books
Discovering God's Will
Experiencing God's Attributes
Experiencing God's Presence
GOD IN YOU—six books and leader's guide
GOD'S DESIGN FOR THE FAMILY—two books
LEARNING TO LIVE—six books
LIFECHANGE—studies of books of the Bible
STUDIES IN CHRISTIAN LIVING—nine books and leader's guide

TOPICAL BIBLE STUDIES

Becoming a Woman of Excellence
God, Man, and Jesus Christ
Growing in Christ—also leader's guide
Homemaking
In His Name
On Holy Ground
Overcoming
Spiritual Fitness—also leader's guide
Think It Through
To Walk and Not Grow Weary

BIBLE STUDIES WITH COMPANION BOOKS

Essentials of Discipleship
The Freedom of Obedience
Friends and Friendship
Honesty, Morality, and Conscience
Marriage Takes More Than Love
The Power of Commitment
The Practice of Godliness
The Pursuit of Holiness

RESOURCES

Explore the Bible Yourself
Leader's Guide for Evangelistic Bible Studies
The Navigator Bible Studies Handbook